Frontline Leadership

Leadership Advice for USAF Junior Officers, Mid-Grade Officers, & NCOs

Written By:
Darrell Moyers, USAF Captain
Michael Parker, USAF Major
Julie Roloson, USAF Major

Contributions from:
Uwe Hartmann, German Army Colonel

Frontline Leadership

Leadership Advice for USAF Junior Officers, Mid-Grade Officers, & NCOs

Darrell Moyers et al.

2020

Carola Hartmann Miles-Verlag

Bibliografische Information der Deutschen Nationalbibliothek

Die Deutsche Nationalbibliothek verzeichnet diese Publikation in der Deutschen Nationalbibliografie; detaillierte bibliografische Daten sind im Internet über www.dnb.de abrufbar.

© 2020 Carola Hartmann Miles-Verlag, Berlin

www.miles-verlag.jimdo.com

email: miles-verlag@t-online.de

Herstellung: Books on Demand, Norderstedt

Printed in Germany

ISBN 978-3-96776-003-3

Table of Contents

Acknowledgments   7

Preface   9

A Brief Note on
Building a Leadership Philosophy   12

Introduction   15

The Success Behind Poor Leadership   17

Pt 1
Practical Lessons for Mid-Level Leaders
Pg 21

Humility and Your Ability to Lead   21

Understand Followership   25

Inspirational Leadership, Empowerment,
and Delegation   31

Be A Mentor   34

Pt 2

From Philosophy to Practice
Pg 38

Talk to Your Boss:
You Need Their Buy-in   39

Lean Back   42

Create a Coalition   47

Identify Dead Weight   55

Return to the Fundamentals of Leadership;
Create the Well-Oiled Machine   57

Optimize & Expand   67

Repeat   69

About The Authors   71

Acknowledgements

Special thanks to my wife Rachel. You make me want to be a better man in everything that I do. You have shown me what it is to truly care for others, both as a leader of our home and of our Airmen.

Thank you to my mentors, Maj Michael Parker and Lt Col Taylor Herron. You have taught me some of my most valuable leadership lessons, both through example and in giving me enough rope to learn tough lessons the hard way. Thank you for allowing me room to fail while showing me how to succeed.

- *Darrell Moyers*

Preface

This document came about from a lunch-break discussion among Air Force Captains and Majors. One of the Majors, Julie Roloson, was about to take her first Squadron command. Julie, naturally anxious to do well, was soliciting advice from her fellow officers on what makes a good Squadron Commander. Julie's approach was novel; she was soliciting advice for how to lead a squadron from the bottom-up, not the top-down; she was asking advice not from fellow Squadron Commanders but from those that have spent the entirety of their careers under them. More Commanders should be like Julie.

Too many Commanders focus on how they can lead their squadron. While the squadron is indeed seen to be 'led' by a Squadron Commander, in practice, a Commander merely vectors their squadron and directs its leaders along that vector. A Commander who involves themselves in the everyday workings of the nitty-gritty in their command will quickly be labeled as a micro-manager. A good Squadron Commander leads the officers of their squadron by enabling those officers to lead the Squadron's Airmen (the embodiment of the squadron) towards the goal of the Commander. Therefore, to say that a Squadron Commander leads a squadron is a flawed statement; a Commander leads Lieutenants, Captains, and Majors, who in turn lead the squadron.

Our discussion with Julie quickly converged on this point. The real value of a leader is determined by how well that leader enables those under him or her to lead, be it a Lieutenant Colonel over Majors and Captains, a Captain over Lieutenants and Non-Commissioned Officers (NCOs), or NCOs over Airmen. The measure of a leader is not how well they accomplish a given task – that is management. A true leader creates other leaders.

To that end, a few members of our lunch-time gathering decided to co-author a document aimed at advising the Air Force's officers and NCOs who are at the frontlines of leadership, those who actually share office space with Airmen. In our research, we discovered that while the Air University has published a book for Squadron Commanders (*Commanding an Air Force Squadron in the Twenty-First Century*), there are surprisingly few resources for advising those of us without a command pin. Furthermore, upon reviewing *Commanding an Air Force Squadron in the Twenty-First Century*, we were surprised to learn how Commander-centric it was written. It focuses heavily on advising Squadron Commanders on how they – themselves – should lead, but offers very little in the way of advice for how to utilize the officers within a command. This article asserts that the premise of Commander centric leadership is a flaw in the existing literature circulating throughout the Air Force.

In that context, this work took on a secondary role, to not only provide junior officers some direction for leadership at their level, but also to complement *Commanding an Air Force Squadron in the Twenty-First Century*. It is our hope that this article will help Commanders gain perspective on how they should lead through the officers under them, and possibly provide a template for commanders to mentor and grow junior leaders.

Our goal is to do so without the platitudes offered within the advice of higher grades (although we reference them when appropriate). With respect to senior officers, they are far detached from the cynicism, struggles, hopes, and realities of the lower grades. While not without value, a General Officer's experience as a Lieutenant was the experience of another officer, in another lifetime, in another Air Force. Our goal is to provide that bottom-up perspective Julie was looking for in hopes it may rectify some of the perceived leadership flaws in the Air Force's officer corps.

-   *Captain Darrell Moyers, Air Force Flight Commander*

A Brief Note on Building a Leadership Philosophy

Leadership is a craft. Those of you who have spent any time studying or practicing leadership know that it is exceedingly difficult to define. Whatever definition you decide to subscribe to, you will find that its practice is vulnerable to a multitude of circumstance. Leadership is not static. Your thoughts on leadership may change from the time that you lead your first small team to the time that you lead a squadron or a wing. We, the authors of this work, are handing you our collective philosophy to help start you in the right direction. For those who have already started, we hope to grant you a useful perspective that may bolster your own philosophy or grow the leadership of those under you.

Early on into the Air Command and Staff College course, in one of the many pre-command checklists floating around, there is a small note that references building a leadership philosophy. This is not to be confused with the vision and mission statement of a unit. Instead, this is a reflection of who you are as a leader. Generally speaking, this is a list of approximately ten bullet points, taking up no more than a single page of paper. While the end product may not seem like much, it is a reflection of the leadership strategies, philosophies, and lessons learned and acquired through a multitude of sources and experiences over a person's time in the Air Force. It provides the author with self-reflection, and (if published) opens a level of transparency to those being led. Early leadership opportunities give a chance for your officers to develop and test the foundations of this leadership philosophy; follow-on opportunities provide a chance for that philosophy to grow and evolve.

No two people will have the same leadership philosophy because such a philosophy is central to who a leader is as a person. As such, when you sit down to define your philosophy, it may not vary greatly as you go from unit to unit or position to position. When you develop your leadership philosophy, take the time to reflect on the type of leaders who have influenced you (both good and bad) and the type of leader that you want to be (and do not want to be). Write down a list of all of the leadership clichés you have come across, all the leadership quotes you have heard or have been forced to memorize. Write down the key lessons you have taken from the leaders that inspired you. Ensure that you also think about the leaders that you did not agree with, and promised yourself that you would never be like. Then take a look at that list and start highlighting the ones that strike both positive and negative chords within you.

The next step is to put these thoughts into your own words. Do not let it be a regurgitation of someone else's ideas. Do not simply write down the core values; those are expected to be inherent in everyone's actions and do not need to be restated in your leadership philosophy. Instead, use your leadership philosophy as your brand, as a document that you consistently reference when making the hard decision. Use your philosophy to guide lines of effort in pursuit of your unit's vision. Check how comfortable you are talking about and promoting it. Take the time to make sure that you are following and holding yourself to it, even amongst the daily churn. Ultimately, continue to hone your craft.

- *Major Julie Roloson, Air Force Squadron Commander*

Introduction

To every man there comes in his lifetime that special moment when he is figuratively tapped on the shoulder and offered that chance to do a very special thing, unique to him and fitted to his talents. What a tragedy if that moment finds him unprepared or unqualified for that which would be his finest hour.[1]

- Winston Churchill

Good leadership is a tricky thing to define without the use of cliché-ridden platitudes. Such platitudes may, at times, provide momentary feelings of inspiration, but be found to be hollow in practice. This article aims to give the reader open-eyed insight into what good leadership *looks like*, thereby avoiding the hollowness in trying to define the term. In doing so, the authors provide the reader with frank and open-eyed insight into our experience with leadership and then back up that experience with credible sources. We, the authors, want to speak to you, the reader, the way we would speak to our mentees – the way we would speak to each other. As such, our work carries with it a healthy amount of cynicism,

---

[1] Lorenz, *Lorenze on Leadership: Lessons on Effectively Leading People, Teams, and Organizations,* 7.

blunt statements, and critical views into the Air Force.

To that end, this article begins with a discussion on why bad leaders exist in the Air Force. The existence of poor leaders within the officer and NCO corps is something every service member has knowledge of, but it seems to be taboo to publicly acknowledge poor leaders within the Force. Squadron Officer School sometimes graduates poor leaders, The NCO Academy sometimes graduates poor Leaders, and the Air Command & Staff College sometimes graduates poor leaders. Poor leaders maintaining successful careers is something that is not supposed to happen, but it does; like any disease, it is something that needs to first be acknowledged in order to be addressed.

This article is then broken up into two parts. The intent of the first part is to provide the reader with some practical lessons on good leadership. It does so by targeting certain leadership themes, specifically, humility, followership, empowerment, and mentorship. In this sense, leadership is defined by presenting the sum of its parts; a leader is not one thing; a leader is several things. The second part of this article provides an example for how some key principles of good leadership may be carried out in practice. We want to demonstrate to you what effective leadership principles look like in action. It is one thing to tell someone to lead, it's quite another to offer them something that they can reasonably emulate. In order to do so, we use the example of transitioning into a position of leadership, an experience officers and NCOs[2] will see time and time again.

The Success Behind Poor Leadership

Why discuss negative aspects of leadership at all? Because it's real; it exists every day in our military and it must be addressed… Boiled down, the [symptoms of poor leadership] fall under two cornerstones: Distrust on all levels and self-preservation at all costs. [3]

- Bradley Reilly, USAF Chief Master Sgt

-

The United States Air Force is a tremendous organization that enables some of the nation's finest men and women to accomplish an incredible amount of good around the world. However, for all of its excellence, the organization carries with it its share of shortfalls, including at times the promotion of poor leadership. One of the dark truths about the military is that bad leaders often have successful careers and sometimes the officers that our Airmen place their faith in let them down. You can, in fact, do well as a career minded officer by disregarding

---

[2] **Author's Note:** Henceforth, the terms 'Officers' and 'Non-Commissioned Officers' (NCOs) are used interchangeably. While the language of 'Officers' is primarily used, the lessons in this work are meant to apply to both brackets of leadership.

[3] Reilly, "Eradicating Toxic Leadership."

fundamental leadership principles and by looking out for yourself. An Air Force officer who manages to avoid illegal activities is almost guaranteed to make Major, and one that merely gains the favor of his boss is likely to receive a positive evaluation that pushes him or her even farther up the chain.

This factor often incentivizes a culture of risk aversion in the Force. In this context, not rocking the boat is beneficial to an officer and their superiors. Even if an officer desires to make change, one must often maintain their position to do so and maintain the favor of those above them. As such, a potential leader may be afraid to test the limits of their authority to make change or allow those under them to lead such change. Often risk aversion results in leaders that actively impede the development, imagination, and creativity of their subordinates. The unwillingness of such leaders to move outside of the comfortable status quo creates a system that frustrates those seeking to improve upon that system from within. Those who are brave enough to "go against the flow" may find themselves being dragged back by peers and supervisors alike seeking to maintain the safety and ease of the status quo.

A lack of willingness to take risk, to change the way we do business, everything from the way our leaders think about war to the processes, and then, therefore, a lack of risk in coming up with new and innovative concepts, and a lack of

Frustrating circumstances such as these often push would-be leaders to seek alternative career paths in the civilian realm. A combination of studies on force attrition have repeatedly shown that bad leaders displaying the above qualities are a key reason why the military loses some of its most valuable leadership potential.[5] In short, good leaders leave because they get tired of dealing with the bad ones. That is not to say that all leaders that are "left" are bad; some of the most determined leaders stay to right the wrongs of others. However, this phenomenon does leave the Force with disproportionately more poor leaders than it should have.

Worse still, the hubris of a poor leader can lead them to raise up officers that display similar traits – officers similar to them – while suppressing officers that display conflicting traits. Just as the best

---

[4] Smiljanic, "Transformational Military Leadership - Requirements, Characteristics and Development," 24.

[5] Brandebo, Osterberg, and Berglund, "The Impact of Constructive and Destructive Leadership on Soldier's Job Satisfaction," 1071–73; "Military Leadership Diversity Commission Decision Paper #3: Retention," 44–46, 55–57.

leaders in the Air Force can point to a mentor that helped mold them, a bad leader can be traced back to one (or several) officers that either molded them or did not take responsibility for their behavior. Good leaders create good leaders, and bad leaders create bad leaders. This cycle, along with the development of risk aversion, is one reason why poor leaders survive, and sometimes thrive, in the Air Force.

The success behind poor leadership is why it takes real courage to truly lead. In today's Air Force, a courageous leader is not the one who leads his troops in storming an objective under gunfire (although such an act is clearly courageous). The vast majority of Air Force officers will never find themselves in such a situation. Courageous leadership in today's Air Force can be defined as a willingness to be a good leader despite the politics sometimes being stacked against you. A leader who truly trusts his people risks his career by placing it in his people's hands. A leader who speaks to his superiors frankly risks an unfavorable performance report. A leader who pushes change risks the label of blame if that change results in failure. A leader who seeks to disrupt the status quo risks creating adversaries in those who favor it.

Often, it is easier to be a poor leader than it is to be a good and courageous leader. This article is for those who desire to be the latter. Do you want to be a successful Air Force officer or a good leader?

Sometimes you can have both and sometimes you have to choose. This article offers leadership-minded advice, not career guidance. It is the hope of the authors that, when given a choice, more Air Force officers will choose the harder path, the embodiment of which is taking care of people, encouraging change, fostering mentorship, and, above all, growing more good leaders.

Practical Lessons for Mid-level Leaders

Part 1

Humility and Your Ability to Lead

Humility and leadership go hand in hand. However, this does not mean that a leader must be meek. Humility requires empathy, self-awareness, and emotional intelligence, all of which are strengths. Far more strength is required from a leader who seeks to keep their emotions under control than it does to simply give in to the moment.

Own your Airmen and empathize with them. Many of the people you lead will be presented with very real and tragic life challenges, sometimes of their own making. At times, it will be for you to judge their actions and act accordingly as their supervisor. Other times, you must approach them without judgement, wrap an arm around them, and help them weather the storm. Take ownership of your Airmen, but know that they do not belong to you. Own them the way you own your mother, your father, your sister, or your brother. It is okay to say "my Airmen." If it is obvious that you are a leader who has their interests at heart, they will see it and know what you mean by such a statement. Own their careers, own their successes, and own their failures. You must also own their families; you owe their families an explanation for every impact you make on their lives.

As a young Flight Commander, my First Sergeant revealed to me that one of my Airmen was facing a Court Martial and possibly a long prison sentence. To me, it did not matter if my Airmen was guilty or innocent – he was "my Airman." He was facing something life changing and it was my duty to be there for him. I showed up to every trial date and made sure he and his parents were greeted with a familiar face every day. Upon hearing the jury say the words "not guilty," his mother broke into tears and hugged me. I am not ashamed to say that I teared up as well. In that moment I realized I was "theirs" as much as he was "mine." His mother still asks how I am doing today.

- Captain Darrell Moyers, Air Force Flight Commander

Have a realistic view of yourself as a leader. Every officer thinks they deserve to be in the "Top Third" of their peer group. Simple math: Over half of the officers in the Air Force are in the bottom 51%; the chances are much higher you are in the bottom half of leaders than in the top 30%. Given that the spots in the top 10% are typically taken up by those with PH.Ds, multiple Distinguished Graduate accolades, <u>and</u> service level awards, chances are better that you are more likely in the "Bottom Third" than in the "Top Third." Everyone has room to grow, and if someone else is not routinely pointing out where that room is as your career unfolds, you are being done a disservice. If you are not seeking this information out, then you are doing yourself a disservice. Demand feedback from those you serve under and from those you serve over. Find out where your weaknesses are, embrace them, and improve upon them.

Know that being an officer grants you no special reverence. The words "yes sir" can come in several different tones and carry a multitude of subtext. The phrase "your Airmen look up to you," is only true in certain circumstances; more likely your Airmen are looking at you to see what acceptable behavior is in your eyes. For those of you who wear rank on your shoulders instead of on your sleeves, the only difference between you and an NCO is that you went to college; it is unlikely your college experience made you a better leader. The best officers find ways to show their reverence for their Airmen, not the other way around.

Unless you are on G-Series orders, your authority is an illusion. Ask yourself what you would do if an Airmen told you to "kick sand" after you gave them a legitimate order. Picture yourself in front of the preponderance of your unit. You could run the act of insubordination up the chain, you could go back to your office and issue paperwork, but *you cannot do anything* in that moment except turn red. Understand that this can happen at anytime, and be humbled by it. You are leading independent adults with different (sometimes with more) life experience than you. They may have signed a Term of Service or an enlistment, but every day they *choose* to follow your orders. You need them more then they need you.

Keep your ego in check and be willing to admit when you are wrong. This will go a long way in presenting a positive image and help you communicate effectively with your team; no one wants to need to circumvent their boss's ego in order to have a frank discussion. This concept also applies to what the Air Force "owes" you. Some officers feel as though they have been cheated after a bad assignment, a board choosing another candidate, or being passed over for an award. Sometimes you will work very hard for a thing which may not manifest in the way you had hoped. This happens to everyone, and the Air Force will take care of you, but it does not owe you any of the specific aspirations that you are hoping for. In times such as these, maintain control of your emotions. Mistakes, even emotional ones, are normal. Be willing to correct yourself when they happen and make amends with anyone they may have affected.

Early in my career, I applied for a development program [and]I had confidence that I would be accepted, so not seeing my name on the list came as a shock. To make matters worse, another officer in my squadron did make the cut. Inwardly, I withdrew from the organization and walked around several days feeling hurt and angry. Eventually, though, I realized that the Air Force only owed me the opportunity to compete. On the day the board met, my records did not meet its standards. Whose fault was that? Mine—no one else's. I put the issue behind me and embraced my squadron mate. This experience taught me the negative effect of allowing my ego to dominate my actions—specifically, my failure to realize that the Air Force had not promised to select me for the program. It did, however, guarantee me equitable consideration and fair competition. I should have expected nothing else.[6]

- *Stephen Lorenz, USAF General Ret*

Understand Followership

In the military, leadership and followership overlap so much so that the terms are nearly synonymous. It is the duty of every service member to carry out the legal orders of those appointed over them, often utilizing the teams of men and women

---

[6] Lorenz, *Lorenze on Leadership: Lessons on Effectively Leading People, Teams, and Organizations*, 6.

assigned under them. Without a clear understanding of a boss's intent, one cannot lead those under them toward its execution. In order to be a good leader, one must also be a good follower. This does not mean one must always agree with their superior or dogmatically carry out their every suggestion. However, followership does mean being clear on your boss's intent, providing them honest feedback, and giving them your support. Give to your boss what you would have your Airmen give to you.

Understanding your boss's intent is the core of good followership. At times that intent may be vague (he or she may want you to handle the details), and at other times it may be more specific. Ask questions and get on the same page. You and your boss are part of a team and everyone on the team should be clear with what the plan is. Often, young officers hear what they think the boss wants and then charge towards that objective, more anxious to impress the boss with quick results than to risk looking foolish with follow-up questions. Always ask questions. Asking questions will show your boss that you are paying attention and can think critically about a problem set. Doing so will also provide them with immediate feedback on how effectively they are conveying their intent.

While I was deployed to ISAF HQ there were a million examples of this happening, especially at the staff level. Frequently we would have a senior commander make a vague

Feedback is critical to effective followership. Give it to your boss and demand it from your people. Leaders are people and sometimes people make bad decisions; no one is infallible. A good practice is to create an inner circle with the top members of your team. Put decisions in front of them and ask them what they think. Do not put the decision on them, but gather their input. At best, they will provide you with wisdom for which to modify your path or provide you with a sample of how the rest of your team may react to your decision. At the very least, you will show your team that you value two-way communication. Either scenario is worth your time.

Likewise, have the courage to provide feedback to your boss. Sometimes it is appropriate to do so during round-table discussions (officers meeting for example) and other times it will be more appropriate to provide feedback behind closed doors. You may provide your boss with a critical insight they did not consider, or you may find out there is more going on behind the decision than you realized.

I was sitting in a staff meeting and the Squadron Commander asked how one of his initiatives was being received by the Airmen. He went around the table and asked each staff member in turn. All responded with "great." When he got to me, I told him that the initiative had a good intent but was becoming one of many drains on the Airmen's time, and, therefore, was seen as a burden by the Airmen. The room was silent for a moment and the boss thanked me and asked me to see him after. In his office, he and I went over the initiative's implantation – as a team. From then on out, my boss privately sought my council on several of his initiatives. We had a great relationship built on communication, mutual respect, and trust.

- *Captain Darrell Moyers, Air Force Flight Commander*

In public, practice leadership loyalty. Occasionally, unpopular decisions will be made or the commander will direct something that you may not personally agree with. While you should respectfully discuss those opinions with the commander, publicly you must execute and support (as long as it is legal, moral, ethical, and safe). That means getting behind those decisions. Once you have clarified and discussed that decision with your boss, their final decision must become *your* decision. Saying things such as, "okay everyone, the squadron commander decided we have to have an exercise this Friday. I know it is silly, but just do it," will not only destroy your relationship with your commander, it will also erode your leadership image with your subordinates. Instead, own the decision. Articulate the news in a manner such as, "okay everyone, we are doing an exercise this Friday." However, make sure you understand the decision. Your Airmen may ask why; you will not be able to own a decision unless you know the "why" behind it.

The most challenging time to be a good follower is when working for a poor leader. A Commander who shuts down feedback, criticizes follow-up questions, and hinders two-way communication can be very demoralizing to a leadership team. As an officer, when working for a bad leader, it is still important to practice all of the above followership principles, even when it would be much easier not to. The principle reason is to take care of your people. Better that you suffer some amount of chastisement than your Airmen suffer the consequences of misunderstanding the Commander's intent. Handle such situations as delicately as possible, but at the end of the day, you still owe your boss clear feedback and communication – bad leader or not. Bad leaders will pass on with time. Until then, do your part as a good follower, provide your people top-cover, and grow the leaders and followers under you.[7]

---

[7] Reilly, "Eradicating Toxic Leadership."

Inspirational Leadership, Empowerment, and Delegation

Inspiring your troops is as easy as enabling them to create change and build morale. The ability to give charismatic speeches can certainly help an officer seeking to motivate their troops, but even the most charismatic voices will be ignored without the appropriate follow through. The act of empowerment requires no grand oration and, done right, will continuously endure. Although it may be easier to say "no," a good leader finds ways to say "yes" when his or her people bring them initiatives. Empowering one's team to make a difference will drive the most powerful and accepted change an organization is capable of experiencing. A good leader should not only be a catalyst for change, but also an advocate for it.[8] A top-tier leader provides the necessary tools, a general direction, and the left and right limits, but also allows their people to take the team to the end state.[9] One of the true measures of leadership skill is how capable that leader is in handing over leadership to those they lead.[10]

---

[8] Lewinska, "The Role of Communication in Military Leadership," 40.

[9] Hedlund et al., "Tacit Knowledge in Military Leadership: Evidence of Construct Validity," 2.

[10] Canning, "Empowering Communities Through Inspirational Leadership," 44–45.

Delegation is a big part of empowerment. Mid-level officers love to tell junior officers how much free time those in the lower grades have and how all that "free time" evaporates once promotion occurs. For the most part, this a sentiment that reflects the reality in the Air Force. The disparity in workload occurs because many leaders do not feel comfortable delegating to the lower grades. There is very little reason behind why a Major should be in his office until 1800 every day when he has five Captains and Lieutenants under him going home at 1500. Such a Major is not properly utilizing his re-

---

[11] Lorenz, *Lorenze on Leadership: Lessons on Effectively Leading People, Teams, and Organizations,* 5–6.

sources and is also doing his subordinate officers a disservice.

There are far too many junior officers that feel underutilized and far too many mid-grade officers that take on too much. The Major in the above example would do better to teach his subordinates vital skills (award package writing, decoration writing, OPR/EPR editing, managing taskers, etc.), share the work load, and show the younger officers that they have what it takes to move on to the next grade.[12] The Major would then be able maintain a reasonable work schedule and his junior officers would gain vital knowledge and experience. There are few junior officers who would turn down the opportunity to peek behind the curtain and take part in a greater leadership role. Research shows that an increase in responsibility correlates with increased job satisfaction amongst young leaders.[13] Young leaders who are more invested in their roles are more likely to take their leadership duties seriously and grow to be better leaders. Embrace those hungry for responsibility, teach them, and trust them with important tasks. The best leaders make more leaders.

Proper delegation comes with both responsibility and authority. It is important that the person

---

[12] Guenzi and Ruta, *Leading Teams: Tools and Techniques for Successful Team Leaders from the Sports World*, 52.

[13] Brandebo, Osterberg, and Berglund, "The Impact of Constructive and Destructive Leadership on Soldier's Job Satisfaction," 1069.

who is being delegated to understands that they speak with the authority of the leader when carrying out an assigned task. It can be extremely frustrating for a subordinate to be assigned a task but not be given the tools required to see that task to fruition. Delegation also comes with trust. Trust that the authority that comes with delegation will not be abused, but also trust in the discretion of the person being delegated to. Research has shown that trust in subordinate decision-making directly correlates with leadership effectiveness.[14] At times, the members of your team may need to call an audible. The alternative path that they take from the one assigned may not be the one that the leader would have chosen. However, it is important that such discretion is encouraged so long as the leader's intent is being pursued. Trust your team, let them know you have faith in their decisions, and watch them come up with innovative methods for carrying out your intent.[15]

Be A Mentor

Valuable mentorship is an elusive gift in the Air Force. If you are lucky enough to find a good mentor, do all you can to maintain that relationship.

---

[14] Velsor, McCauley, and Ruderman, *Handbook of Leadership Development*, 99.

[15] Mance, Pearce, and Sims, "The Ins and Outs of Leading Teams: An Overview," 180.

Mentorship is one of those things that the Air Force touts but has no way of really fostering. This is unfortunate as many of the skills that a junior officer is expected to develop do not come from the Professional Military Education (PME) system. PME may spend a few days showing a young officer how to write a bullet, but does not have the resources or time to make that officer a proficient writer. Nor does PME make an officer proficient in award routing, knowledgeable in training opportunities, or skilled in funding allocation. PME may expose a young officer to some of the parts and pieces of successful organizational and career management, but an officer is expected to gain expertise elsewhere; they are expected to get it from would-be mentors. The lucky few who find these mentors gain an invaluable edge over their peers.

Two types of mentorship exist in the Air Force, formal and informal. Formal mentorship is valuable in its own right, but not a career enlightening experience. Formal mentorship is the type a subordinate receives from their boss during annual feedback sessions. It often resembles a cookie-cutter approach to advising a junior officer on their career path. Such advisement often carries little individualistic value. It focuses on advice such as "volunteer more," "further your education," "you're doing well." It is likely an individual meeting with a formal mentor has a pretty good idea of what they are going to be told before the mentor makes their first utterance. As such, many junior officers do not know where they stand in comparison to their peers and lack a general understanding of their strengths and weaknesses as leaders. Unfortunately, because formal mentorship is easy, and even easier to gloss over, it can become the go-to for many supervisors. As such, this is the majority of mentorship that young officers receive.

Informal mentorship is akin to water in the desert. While formal leadership lasts so long as the formal relationship between supervisor and supervisee is maintained, informal mentorship can continue for years as a continuous process.[16] This type of mentorship is informal only in the sense that it is not mandatory and can be akin to a relationship between older and younger siblings. An informal mentor is someone who is more experienced than the mentee and genuinely wants to develop them into a better leader as they progress through their career. This includes vital skills such as writing, but also includes discussions on general life lessons, leadership challenges, and career advice. An informal mentor invests significant time and energy into a person that they will not directly receive dividends from. As such, it is far more difficult to be an informal mentor than a formal one; however, such a mentor provides far more for the long-term development of the Air Force.

---

[16] Velsor, McCauley, and Ruderman, *Handbook of Leadership Development*, 77.

A good leader creates good leaders. One of the most effective ways of making good leaders is through solid mentorship. As stated in the *Success Behind Poor Leadership* section of this work, all good leaders can point to that solid mentor that helped them along the way. Find a good mentor if you can and foster that relationship. Mentorship requires a two-way relationship; a mentor cannot be expected to chase down their mentee, they can only be expected to be available to a mentee in need. As you progress in your career, attempt to take young officers under your wing whenever possible. You will not be able to be a full-time mentor to every subordinate you come across, but over the course of your career, you should pick up one or two that regularly look to you for advice.

Mentorship can be extra work, but it is one of the most rewarding leadership experiences available to you in the Air Force. Leadership positions come and go. You can lead a team towards a fantastic initiative and the next officer that backfills you can take that team in a completely different direction. If you desire to have a lasting impact on the Air Force – if you truly want to leave your mark – leave it on the next generation. People forget squadron initiatives, but they do not forget the leaders that made a lasting impact on their careers.

From Philosophy to Practice

Part 2

What follows is a general methodology for those who are transitioning into a leadership position. It is far from all inclusive; each leadership role is contextual.[17] It is also not meant to be a *how to*. The primary intent of this strategy is to demonstrate effective leadership principles in action. It's one thing to tell a leader to have a vision, it's quite another to show them how a vision might be carried out. The secondary purpose is to provide basic advice to those seeking to enter positions of leadership, those with authority to lead change. While a certain amount of leadership can happen at all levels, this methodology is primary focused on the roles of Flight Commanders, Officers in Charge, Section Chiefs, Non-Commissioned Officers in Charge, Senior Intelligence Officers, Directors of Operations, and, to some extent, Squadron Commanders. This guide recommends a seven-phase approach to taking on a position of leadership: Talk to Your Boss, Lean Back, Create a Coalition, Find Dead Weight, Return to Fundamentals, Optimize & Expand, and Repeat.

---

[17] Cohen, *Supreme Command: Soldiers, Statesmen, and Leadership in Wartime*, 217.

Talk to Your Boss:
You Need Their Buy-in

This phase may seem overly straightforward. However, the larger or busier a unit is, the easier this concept is to overlook. Generally, all new officers to a unit receive some type of meet-and-greet. What is recommended here is to get on the boss's calendar, find out what their intent is, and discuss how they think your position can meet that intent. Do this immediately; do not wait until a complete changeover or to get settled. This conversation may take place at the same time as the initial feedback, but if the feedback does not provide enough guidance, be prepared to ask questions to receive that guidance. Everything you absorb about your position should be viewed through the lens of intent. The best way to successfully implement any form of change is to get the boss's backing; the best way to do that is to match up your initiatives, and those of your Airmen, with your commander's intent. Your boss may be focused on resiliency, innovation, or expanding operations. That intent will tell you where to take your team and likely give you the authority and resources to get there. It is imperative that you understand your boss's vision as it will shape your own.[18]

---

[18] Smith, *Commanding an Air Force Squadron in the Twenty-First Century: A Practical Guide of Tips and Techniques for Today's Squadron Commander*, 7.

Such a conversation is likely to give insight into what the relationship with your boss will be, and how much latitude he or she is going to extend to you. Figure out what each other's leadership styles are and encourage your boss to share an open dialogue with you. Ask them directly if they have any quirks that set them off, or any communication styles they prefer. Understand that this dialogue is unequal, but it is an unequal dialogue in which both sides must express their views equally and bluntly in order to form an effective team. The dialogue is "unequal" in that the final authority of your boss is unquestioned publicly and wholly ambiguous.[19]

The openness of this type of dialogue will allow you to hold your boss accountable while also working in tandem with him or her. Holding your boss accountable allows you to let him or her know when your team is being held back (possibly by themselves or their staff) and where you need help. The success of your boss is likely dependent upon

---

[19] Cohen, *Supreme Command: Soldiers, Statesmen, and Leadership in Wartime*, 209.

your own. Your boss has the incentive to support you or get out of your way once they know to do so.[20] If the boss says they support something, or is going to do something, remind them of it, and expect them to do the same with you.

We will still need men and women in uniform to call things as they see them and tell their subordinates and superiors alike what they need to hear, not what they want to hear… If as an officer – listen to me very carefully – if as an officer you don't tell blunt truths or create an environment where candor is encouraged then you've done yourself and the institution a disservice[21]

- Robert Gates as Secretary of Defense at West Point

You and your boss should see your relationship as a team, respect each other's decisions, publicly back each other, settle disputes privately, and, above all, trust one another. Without trust you will not confide in each other. This confidence is necessary to understand deeper levels of intent from which you both must act. This does not mean that your boss needs to agree with everything you want to do, but the two of you need to be on the same

---

[20] Smith, *Commanding an Air Force Squadron in the Twenty-First Century: A Practical Guide of Tips and Techniques for Today's Squadron Commander*, 48.
[21] Gates, *Duty: Memoirs of a Secretary at War*, 134.

page as to where you intend to take your team and how you intend to get there.

Lean Back

Take time to survey the flock, and do so with humility. Be prepared to realize that any preconceptions you had about the leadership position you are about to enter could be entirely wrong. Use two weeks or two months, whatever it takes, to get a comprehensive view of the unit. It is important to ignore "the emails" to the greatest extent possible during this time. Get plugged in by doing and learn about the unit's climate. You may have been in several positions and seen several units, but you have not seen *this* one. Find opportunities to let Airmen show you how much you do not know. The better leaders tend to "admit ignorance or fear than to display false knowledge or bravado. And candidly admitting [short falls] is key to building confidence in your honesty."[22] Take your predecessor's changeover with a grain of salt and learn about the unit for yourself; the person you replaced has but one perspective.

Learn what everyone's jobs are. Learn the roles of the different shops in your unit and the duties of the individuals within them. Officers are not meant to be experts, but good leaders know where

---

[22] McChrystal, *My Share of the Task*, 393.

42

to find the experts. When confronted with a question you do not know the answer to, be able to walk the inquisitor over to the person that does. Physically putting the two in contact with one another displays a willingness to contribute time and effort to someone coming to you for information, and shows a reverence for the person who has the information. The time you take to do this recovered later when future inquiries are directed at the expert and not at you.

Start looking for what does not make sense. Ask at all ranks and keep notes. Survey your Airmen, your NCOs, your Officers, and your leadership. Often, the best or most innovative solutions come from the lowest levels of the organization. That 3-level Airmen that is only 6 weeks out of tech school has a mind, has an opinion, and should have a voice. Make special note of areas brought up by your Airmen that overlap. If one group doesn't understand the legitimate reason *why* something occurs, you owe them a reason or you owe it to them to get rid of that something.

The challenge for a supreme leader lies not in choosing at which level of guidance or abstraction to function, but rather in integrating the details with the grand themes, in understanding the forest by examining certain copses and even individual trees with great care.[23]

- Elliot A. Cohen, Author of Supreme Command

Examine what the workload looks like in your unit. Find out who is carrying the load. Are the Airmen staying late, the Flight Commanders taking on too much? Is your leadership team the first there and the last to leave? No section should carry a disproportionate amount of the burden. The Air Force will get its due out of you and your troops; do not let your team get burned out in garrison. Airmen quality of life and CGO burn-out is a major contributor to why the Air Force bleeds so much talent back into the civilian market.[24] The officer corps is particularly guilty of this sin, when instead, they should be setting the tone. The culture of "time invested equates to productivity" can be extremely pervasive but is flawed. Leaders who are *doing* too much are not *leading* enough. If you or your people are consistently working beyond normal duty hours, be critical of how the time during duty hours is being spent. Understand what leading from the front is and is not.

---

[23] Cohen, *Supreme Command: Soldiers, Statesmen, and Leadership in Wartime,* 212.

[24] Langley, "Occupational Burnout and Retention of Air Force Distributed Common Ground System Intelligence Personnel," 27–28.

44

The actions of you and your officers resonate across your unit.

Take time to socialize with your Airmen. The adage that *leaders don't have to be liked* is somewhat a fallacy and Officers who use this phrase are often times not liked. However, one must be genuine; do not pretend, your people will always see through a façade with time. This does not mean you should be overly chummy with your Airmen; you are not their friend. Moreover, the Airmen are not looking for a friend, they are looking for a leader. However, having something resembling a personality goes along way. If you are going to lead men and women, then you need them to follow you because they want to do so, not because they have to. You need Airmen to respect you for your leadership, not pay homage to you for your rank or authority. Airmen generally respect leaders they like, can identify with, and that they find approachable. In the end, it is really about respect, and it is better to be respected than liked. However, an Airmen is unlikely to respect someone that they detest, and inversely, Airmen will find it hard not to respect someone they have built a bond with. The difference in a troop getting behind your initiatives and limiting their activities to what they are specifically directed to do correlates highly with their opinion of you.[25]

---

[25] Dobelli, *The Art of Thinking Clearly*, 65.

This is a particularly salient point for officers of lower rank. It goes without saying that a Colonel inherently garners more respect than a Lieutenant from a group of Airmen. Younger officers do not benefit from the same halo-effect[26] that senior officers do. The lower your rank, the higher you must climb this ladder. It is difficult for a Captain who has been in the service for four years to convince a Technical Sergeant who has been in for eight years that he should follow the Captain for reasons outside of rank. The farther you are down the ladder and the more you work with your Airmen on a daily basis, the more your Airmen will humanize you and the more you will get to know them. You are no longer an unknown, no longer the mysterious authority figure; you are the Captain that stumbled over an attempt at an inspirational speech, or the Lieutenant who spilled coffee in his own lap last week. You do not need to be perfect to be an effective leader, in fact, showing these vulnerabilities and

---

[26] Dobelli, 114. Halo Effect: Falsely ascribing success, respect, or reliability in multiple areas due to a remarkable trait in a single area.

46

your humanity will make you a better leader Do not throw customs and courtesies out the window and maintain force discipline, but ensure your Airmen feel comfortable talking to you. You're part of a team.

The best leaders I've seen have an uncanny ability to understand, empathize, and communicate with those they lead.[27]

- General Stanley McChrystal

Create a Coalition

Create a vision from your observations in the Lean Back phase. This vision should be straightforward, clear, and attainable. It needs to be reachable in a relatively short period of time (less than a year), but not so easily reached that achieving it becomes a hollow victory. Your vision can adapt over time and become one with a longer time horizon, but a vision with a goal that is perceived to be attainable (hence a short time horizon) will garner more support. Any change you try to push forward across your team will require some sort of sacrifice from those you lead, be it a small effort or a large one. People will not sacrifice for change "even if they are unhappy with the status quo, unless they think the potential bene-

---

[27] McChrystal, *My Share of the Task*, 392.

fits are attractive and unless they really believe that a transformation is possible."[28] The below vision is easily understood, attainable, of obvious benefit to your team, and sets the foundation for the next vision (bring them closer to their families and each other). This is the vision this paper's leadership strategy is oriented towards:

Simple Vision

Create the white space needed to professionally develop our Airmen, bring them closer to their families, and bring them closer to each other.

Get your trigger pullers on the same page with your vision. You cannot execute your initiatives alone; your frontline CGOs and NCOs are vital. Explain to them how that vision correlates with your boss's intent and give them the authority to execute that intent. It is incredibly empowering to an NCO or young officer to be told that they have your authority to execute taskings as they see fit (as long as it's in the realm of intent). New initiatives often fail when the team, "even though they embrace a new vision, feel disempowered."[29] As long as they can explain why the decisions they make match up to the team's vision, back those decisions. If it is a decision you do not agree with, still back it, but coach the

---

[28] Kotter, *Leading Change*, 9.
[29] Kotter, 10.

48

member after the fact. This allows them to own the task as if it was their own, shows them you trust them; this is a strategy that can be incredibly unifying to a team under a new leader.

Encourage dissent, especially early on. Pull objections and ideas out of your team, take a minute to reflect on those comments, and decide if you need to course correct. However, keep the team locked on the primary vision; table extraneous ideas (good idea fairies) for the next round of initiatives. You cannot do everything at once. Focus on the primary objective first; your new team is going to need that win. One of the key contributors in the infamous McChrystal affair (published article in which General McChrystal was critical of the President) during the Obama administration was how the President's team was unclear on what the objectives were. This situation left a certain amount of toxicity amongst the team.[30] Such divisiveness ultimately spilled into a *Rolling Stone* article, resulting in McChrystal's dismissal.[31] Make sure your team knows what the plan is, incorporate their inputs and then execute. Categorize new initiatives that come up along the way and hit them on the next round.

Set up short-term wins and get your boss behind your vision. As stated in the Talk to Your Boss section of this paper, your ability to accomplish

---

[30] Woodward, *Obama's Wars*, 213.
[31] Woodward, 371–72.

anything meaningful will be severely limited without your boss being on board. The vision provided in this paper is flexible enough to be framed around most goals your boss may direct you towards. You can accomplish whatever your boss is after once you have the maneuverability to get there. Your boss can provide you top cover, which will be essential when driving change; when you shake trees, things sometimes fall out of them. Your boss is also one of your easiest and fastest ways to garner your team some short-term wins en route to the success of a long-term vision.

Without short-term wins, teams often become complacent, and, at worst, begin to passively resist change.[32] You can, and should, tout the successes of individuals; a pat on the back goes along way. However, you can supercharge that impact by routing that praise through the next echelon of command. Be straightforward and ask your boss to present one of his coins to one of your troops for a job well done. Coins are an underutilized tool; your boss does not pay for them (Squadron Commanders and above have unit funded coins), and they can go a long way in strengthening EPRs, arguments for promotion recommendations, and awards packages. This also shows your boss that you are serious about taking care of your people and places at their feet examples of how your team is executing their intent.

---

[32] Kotter, *Leading Change*, 12.

To the same end, look for excuses to issue mid-tour or single act decorations and then push strongly for them. This is a terribly under-utilized tool many Officers have easy access to. Mid-tours are easily justified if you are paying attention to what your team has been up to, and Air Force Achievement medals can be approved by Squadron Commanders (If you are a Squadron Commander reading this, and your boss has not threatened to take this power away from you for over-use, then you are doing it wrong). Some shy away from these tools for fear of push back or fear of "cheapening" their value, but both are poor excuses for not using a leadership tool. Fear of push back equates to mild cowardice and given the fact that Officers are on 2-3 year assignment rotations, out-of-sync with their troops, your ability to cheapen an award is limited. In supporting your troops in this fashion, you are not only boosting their pride, moral, and trust in their unit to look out for them, you are also padding their EPRs, awards packages, and subsequently, their careers.

---

[33] Kotter, 13.

Once word gets out and it becomes obvious you take care of your people, then your collation may just build itself.

Understand who holds the keys to progress in your unit and try to get them on board. Define who controls funds, who can affect manning, who has authority over areas you want to shape, and who can discern if what you are trying to do is legal – especially the First Sergeant. These people can turbo-boost or drag down your initiative quickly. There is always money to be found if you can tap into the right people and frame your initiative properly; doing so will significantly widen the aperture of what you can accomplish for your troops. Your key-holder to manning can not only to get you more people, but can also broaden your Airmens' experience and development through programs such as personnel exchanges and PCAs. Making opportunities like this available can significantly boost morale and create buy-in. Your peers also fall into this category. They have their own social networks and can be a boon or bane to your initiatives. You can likely find avenues around or over any key-holder whom may prove themselves an obstacle to your goals. However, by circumventing a need to do so, you are avoiding significant obstacles these people can place in your path to progress.

A good First Sergeant can access all the keys, yet holds none of them. The Shirt can be your most vital asset for making progress in your initiatives, particularly if such progress is in the interest of your troops. The only person who is likely to care about the welfare of your troops as much as you do is the Shirt; it is, by job description, their first priority.[34] Take everything this paper has mentioned thus far about your boss and apply it to the First Sergeant. Having the trust and backing of your Shirt opens a whole network of contacts and influences, most of which extend beyond your unit. Your Shirt is one of many across your Wing, each of which communicates with and performs an exchange of favors for one another. Help your Shirt do their job by safeguarding the welfare of your troops, and the Shirt will deliver unto you the keys to their network. The Shirt has contacts in Finance, Legal, Civil Engineering, Security Forces, Personnel, and every other aspect of the military institution. This makes them a vital asset in your coalition.

More importantly, your Shirt is a treasure trove of insight and experience. Regardless of your rank, your shirt has far more experience leading and managing the enlisted force than you do. You may be the formal leader of your team, "but he or she, not you, is the most important informal leader."[35] Your Shirt can provide you with a more *plugged-in* perspective on the health and needs of your unit, a

---

[34] Smith, *Commanding an Air Force Squadron in the Twenty-First Century: A Practical Guide of Tips and Techniques for Today's Squadron Commander*, 71.
[35] Smith, 70.

shortcut and alternate perspective to the meaning of the things observed during the Lean Back phase. Additionally, a good Shirt can be a solid confidant and a guiding force when making difficult decisions for your team.

Understand that not everyone is going to be on board with your initiatives. There will be individuals or other teams that impede your path to progress. This may be due to conflicting interests, but most often leaders struggle with passive resistance. An organization that has been getting by on the status quo has likely been straddling the fence of mediocrity for some time. Threatening that balance can give to those within your organization, those that are happy to simply punch in and out every day, incentive to undermine your efforts.[36] This can, in part, be combated by instilling a sense of urgency in your team – as long as it does not also create anxiety across the workforce. A sense of urgency when trying to drive change in an organization is necessary; however, a leader that confuses urgency with anxiety risks encountering strong resistance and reinforcing the status quo.[37] Leading change in a new organization is an uphill effort.

---

[36] Kotter, *Leading Change*, 46.
[37] Kotter, 5.

Identify Dead Weight

Start making whitespace; you need to make room to maneuver. New leadership is notorious for coming in with new initiatives without fully uprooting the old. The piling on of requirements and processes places demands on time. That time typically does not come from the mission, it comes out of the Airmen. Before you can successfully implement something new, you need to weed out something old.

Begin by looking for what does not make sense. Seek out responses such as, "we've always done it this way," and then ask why; maybe it is done that way for a reason or maybe it is complacency. If no one person can give you a full and comprehensive explanation for the "why" of the process, it probably doesn't make sense and likely needs to be terminated. You do not have to fully understand the explanation you are given – you are not the expert – but an expert should be able to explain a process to you in a way that seems reasonable.

Once you find the subject matter expert who can illuminate how a policy, plan, or program makes sense, ask them how it fits in with the boss's stated intent. The policy, plan, or program may have a reason, but it still may rest apart from the grand strategy. Commander's intent is your best weapon for overcoming the inevitable resistance to change and any resulting arguments. If push comes to shove and the issue is brought to the boss, when you are able to explain intent and your adversary cannot, you will win.

Be transparent with your Airmen on what you are doing and why. Your ability to clearly and honestly communicate the *why* is absolutely vital. They may not agree with all your moves, but if they understand why you are making them – in an attempt to serve them – they will respect you for it. This is crucial to later steps in the process when you may need to reclaim some of this coveted whitespace back from your airmen; you will need them to be on board when the workload gets heavy. Keep them in the loop regarding the status of your team's progress. Use a clearly visible whiteboard depicting milestones and use PowerPoint to regularly remind key members what the universal goal is. Doing so will highlight short-term wins, display how much progress has been achieved, and keep your team oriented in the same direction. If you are not making progress on those milestones, take the time to figure out why and reevaluate how they can be accomplished.

After all the easy cuts have been made, find ways to cut deeper. If something is mildly contributing to the mission or to commander's intent, consider cutting it in preparation of replacing it with something more effective. Identify programs that can be lost in the realm of acceptable risk to the mission. Determining acceptable risk may just be a cost-benefit analysis of what new initiative be provided. Communication, both up and down, is vital in this type of maneuver. However, a productive force of four will get more done than an unproductive force of six. The idea of this strategy is to eventually get to a productive force of six, but you may have bring it down to four for a time in order to get there.

Return to the Fundamentals of Leadership; Create the Well-Oiled Machine

Nobody cares how much time you put in; they only care about how smoothly your operation runs. For some reason, it seems that the majority of Air Force officers, especially in the younger grades, believe that the time they put in equates to the quality of work they put out. To this end, they personally take on or micromanage every aspect of their team. This is not only a poor methodology in regards to a healthy work-life balance, but also a poor strategy for effectively leading Airmen. If you do this, you will inadvertently signal to your team that you expect similar behavior out of them, regardless of what contradictory verbal statements you make; a team will infer expectations from the actions of their leader. More importantly, such a leader hoards potential developmental opportunities from their Airmen. The success of a unit "is rarely the work of a single leader: Leaders work best in partnership with other leaders."[38] By understanding how to delegate properly, a cornerstone to effective leadership, you will create leaders to run your team for you. This should be the goal of any great leader – to create and inspire other leaders.

Leaders who are efficiently delegating should essentially be working themselves out of a job. Unfortunately, this is one of the skills Air Force leaders, at all grades, struggle with the most. Air Force commissioning sources, Professional Military Education, and senior leaders fail to instill this trait in young officers. Many feel guilty about delegating or simply do not trust their subordinates to not fail. Leadership is largely delegation; this trait is arguably the most important skill an Air Force leader can practice. Delegation is not the relinquishment of responsibility; it is the passing on of authority. When you delegate, you still own the outcomes, so place your trust well. Effective delegation frees up space for a leader to mentor, advocate, chase funding, polish awards packages, pursue initiatives, coordinate with other agencies, network, and work with troops on personal or family issues. Stop *doing* and start *leading;* focus on people over tasks.

Flatten your team's tasking structure and free up your leaders to lead. Take a hard look at what is on your plate. How much of what you are tasked

---

[38] McChrystal, *My Share of the Task*, 392.

with absolutely needs to be done by you? Show your junior officers how to write and they can review awards before packages get to your desk. Find a fire-and-forget NCO and tell them they are responsible for the team's readiness items. Do one better, tell that NCO to delegate oversight of individual readiness categories to Airmen. Give them the task and the tools to accomplish it. Start distributing everything possible on your plate to the next level of leadership below you. Have that level of leadership do the same, and so on.

I'm going to put these men to the severest tests which I can devise in time of peace. I'm going to start shifting them into jobs of greater responsibility than those they hold now.[39]

- General George C. Marshall

When delegating, it is imperative that your subordinates know precisely what it is that you expect from them. Do not outline how you expect them to accomplish a task; tell them what you expect and let them carry it out. To clarify, "carry it out" and "figure it out," are not the same thing. Be prepared to let things be done in ways other than, or even slower than, you would have them done. Often, leaders equate "my way" as the "right way". When

---

[39] Ricks, *The Generals: American Military Command from World War II to Today*, 35.

you give your team a task to accomplish, as long as they are not doing things dangerously or illegally (again, use the Shirt!), trust them to find their own path. Make sure your Airmen have the tools they need to accomplish the task and lightly coach them along the way. Anything less will discourage your team and possibly result in passive resistance.

Emphasize basic leadership principles to your team members when discussing expectations. Use feedback and evaluations to emphasize leadership, but be sure to clarify what you mean by leadership. Make sure your subordinate leaders are pushing down these expectations to their subordinates. The same work-life balance mentioned at the beginning of this phase holds true for your subordinates. If they are not accomplishing their work within the duty day, they either have too much on their plate, they are not delegating properly, or they are inefficient. In each case, it is your responsibility to balance the matter by clarifying expectations or revaluating how you have distributed tasks.

One thing we've seen in my community is that leadership at the NCO and the younger CGO level has slipped to only mean making sure their troops pass their CDCs, PT tests, and get their EPR on time. It needs to be more than that, and it requires stronger leadership from all levels

\- *Major Julie Roloson, Air Force Squadron Commander*

Set your Airmen up for failure and watch them surprise you. Have you ever heard the adage about the intelligent student who earned poor grades because they were bored with the subject, but put that student in the next higher grade and they end up preforming quite well? Take that same principle and apply it to your Airmen. The population pool of the Air Force is not unlike the civilian world; there are indeed some poor performers you will not be able to motivate. Hold your underperformers accountable, but avoid spending the majority of your time on them. Those folks will ride out their term and then move on to something that better suits their disposition. However, the majority of your underperforming Airmen likely only feel underutilized, are jaded from lack of recognition, or feel disenfranchised in not having had a say. These folks are your greatest untapped resource.

In the end, leadership is all about dealing with human beings – regardless if it happens on the tactical or strategic

-   Colonel Uwe Hartmann, German Army

Put your underperformers in positions of real responsibility. A new opportunity in front of a new boss will give an Airman an incredible jolt of initiative. Do not hand them all of the keys, but give them something with some real risk of failure. Keep in mind that failure has to be something that you are willing to answer for. If you explain to your boss what you are doing and why, coming in late on a few taskings will likely be a nonissue. If, and when, your Airman fails, how you handle that failure will redefine your relationship. Expect them to fail occasionally and coach them with positivity when they do. Such an act will build the Airman's trust in you and encourage them to redouble their efforts. Ask yourself: Did you match that Airman with the right position? Do their skills and strengths match up? Where else could they be tried? If the Airman is failing because he or she are truly disinterested, give the position to another Airman and try again. This will show the unit that the delegation of duty titles, responsibility, and authority are earned. Few join the military to fade into the realm of insignificance; there is work ethic and pride in there somewhere. It is often buried under years of disenfranchisement and jadedness handed to Airmen by poor leadership. Most of your troops want to do well, so let them and trust in the results.

Our Leader development efforts must create the climate for greater trust, and challenge leaders to the point of failure as a way to evaluate character, fortitude, and resiliency of personality in conditions of adversity. Critically, we must collectively

- General Martine E. Dempsey

Reinforce delegation with a new command breakout. A new manning diagram with every Airman's title reflecting their responsibilities will infer a level of authority to the Airmen, demonstrate to the Airmen you are serious about making them part of your leadership, and clearly articulate to the rest of your team to whom they may speak to about a particular issue. For example: Place an NCO in charge of readiness who oversees a SrA of Health, a SrA of Fitness, and a SrA of Training. The SrA in charge of Health would oversee one Airman responsible for ensuring team members are up to-date on their vaccines, and another Airman responsible for ensuring all team members are up to date on their annual dental exams. When your team becomes behind on their vaccines, you ping the NCO, who pings the SrA, who pings their Airman. Different teams will vary; their size may limit how spread out you can make these taskings, and the level of leadership you sit at will dictate what your tasking will look like. Nonetheless, you should attempt to recruit as many members of your team into leadership positions (of some type) as possible. Reinforce the chain and soon the machine will be running itself.

---

[40] Dempsey, "Mission Command," 8.

Regardless of what level of responsibility your team possesses, reinforce the execution of your basic deliverables. This is the engine of the well-oiled machine that you are trying to build. For many levels of leadership this includes: IMR currencies, PT programs, CBT currencies, EPRs/OPRs on time, award package deadlines, currency qualifications, upgrade-training pass rates, and CDC pass rates. These basic deliverables are where your team may draw much of its credibility from. Your team needs basic credibility to convince your boss that they should continue to back your efforts. This is the easiest and fastest way to show relevant success in your transformation efforts.

The execution of basic deliverables may start to sound a bit like management, and to an extent it is. The primary difference is that you as the leader are building programs around leadership fundamentals and putting Airmen in charge of executing the deliverables. Herein, your unit's reputation rides on the shoulders of your Airmen. You should articulate this fact to them and let them own it; inspire them to make the unit/team/flight/squadron their own. Management is also an important complement to leadership; the two are not mutually exclusive and often overlap. You will need both management and leadership to drive your team to success, and, "they must work in tandem... The former keeps the whole process under control, while the latter drives the change."[41] The more Airmen holding a piece of flight responsibility the better. Done correctly, and with enough breadth, Airmen will hold other Airmen responsible for their part in flight success.

Often, and typically dripping with nothing but loft platitudes and bumper sticker clichés, we push the message of 'leadership good, management bad,' or 'leaders motivate from the front and managers drive from the back.' However, management should not be subject to be avoided. It is far better that CGOs learn and utilize GOOD management techniques with their leadership than wait till they are Majors or Lieutenant Colonels to figure out what management is all about

\- *Major Michael Parker, Air Force Senior Intelligence Officer*

Hold your Airmen accountable for their successes as well as their failures. Find a metric to compare them to as a team and give your team a title to live up to (Best Flight in the Squadron, Best Squadron in the Group, Best Team on the Flight). Additionally, publicly recognize individual Airmen within your team wins, all of which will push the short-term wins mentioned in the *Create a Coalition* phase of this document. At the same time, you must also hold your team members accountable for failing to live up to the team's reputation. In the majority of instances, this will likely involve coaching to correction. How-

---

[41] Kotter, *Leading Change*, 60.

ever, failing to displace underperformers can instill a cynical mindset in your Airmen and be counterproductive to your motivating them.

It's imperative that every airman and officer who drives through the gate each morning understands that he or she is essential to the success of the squadron.[42]

- Lieutenant Colonel Jeffry F. Smith, Author of Commanding an Air Force Squadron in the Twenty-First Century

Empower your leaders at every level. The best way to do this is to ensure they understand they have your confidence. Let them know they operate with your authority when carrying out duties you have assigned to them. Give them top-cover and back them up when they encounter resistance. A part of confidence is open dialogue. Take their inputs seriously and demonstrate to them how quickly you can get their ideas up to the boss. Show them tangible effects from their initiatives. Most importantly, give them a voice and take it seriously. Allow them to advise you, and, as long as they are being respectful, leave rank and hubris outside of your conversations. General McChrystal's success with Iraq's most successful Special Operations task

---

[42] Smith, *Commanding an Air Force Squadron in the Twenty-First Century: A Practical Guide of Tips and Techniques for Today's Squadron Commander*, 6.

66

force (TF 714) can be attributed to such empowerment strategies.

[In TF 714] you have got voice… everybody had a voice and so rank didn't matter, age didn't matter, what mattered was the value you added. Did you have value to provide, and if you did, provide it! You have a responsibility to do that. It's not just the commander or the J2 or the J3, it's everybody.[43]

- General Michael Flynn

Optimize & Expand

Reorganize where called for and replace people in underperforming positions. You may have to fire a low-speed NCO and give his job to a high-speed Airman. If this occurs, do so in a respectful way. The idea is not to humiliate the NCO, but to emphasize competence over entitlement. Positions of leadership should be earned when given and continually revalidated through performance. However, before replacing personnel, ask your team if the position needs to be reshaped or redefined. Your direction as to what is to be expected from that position may be as much to blame as the person occupying that position.

---

[43] Shultz, "Military Innovation in War: It Takes a Learning Organization, A Case Study of Task Force 714 in Iraq," 30.

Streamline the process your team has come up with. Ask them: How can we do things we *need to do* better or with less effort? Knock down any obstacles that your Airmen may be facing and constantly reassess your team's leadership fundamentals. Once tasks are efficiently streamlined, the lowest levels of the organization will execute deliverables without being asked. Your goal in this phase is to establish a new culture, or capitalize on the culture your unit already has, through crystal clear expectations and processes. However, it is imperative that your leadership team understands that establishing norms takes time, often meets setbacks, and will be met with resistance. New norms challenge old norms. The longer a norm is in place, the stronger it will be. Therefore, new norms are at a disadvantage. Their establishment requires constant nurturing and encouragement.

Start taking on new projects and take bigger risks. Ambitiously incorporate the new ideas of your Airmen. The whole point of creating the reputation mentioned in the previous phase was to get to this point. Push well-planned initiatives and encourage development of sporadic ones. Create new leaders for new projects. Give special consideration to projects that have the potential to add to the cohesiveness of your team, such as professional development projects, resiliency projects, or e*spirit de corps* projects; pride in the organization translates to pride in the team's product. Accept risk in these projects. Innovation often means more failure than success. Embrace the failures and trust them to lead you to something better than you had before.

We need our squadrons to be aggressively persistent and take risks in the pursuit of new ideas and solutions …Part of the job of leaders is to unleash that brilliance and to create an environment where young folks with good ideas actually can get a hearing. And we can give them some resources and time and energy to allow them to pursue those ideas and see where it goes… We know not every idea is a homerun. If an idea fails, we want it to fail fast and our Airmen to learn even faster. And because we've shown them we believe in their ideas, I want them to keep swinging until we find the answer… they must be supported by leaders who not only remove unnecessary barriers to success, but who also lift up and champion their ideas. [44]

- General David L. Goldfien, Chief of Staff of the Air Force

Repeat

Officer assignments in the Air Force are relatively short lived. Positions with command authority are even shorter. This limited time horizon can inhibit a leader's ability to make significant or lasting changes in a unit. If you are successful in implement-

---

[44] "AF to Fund Squadron Innovation That Improves Mission Effectiveness."

ing the advice in this paper, you should continue to innovate and expand. Use the first six phases as a guideline to re-evaluate your vision and create whitespace for more innovation. Likely, your execution of the *Repeat* phase of this strategy will occur in your next leadership position. The main point of this work is to pass on a philosophy of making better leaders across the Air Force. Not just with you, the reader, but in the Airmen you will lead, be they enlisted or officer. Good people leave the Air Force because of bad leadership. The Army Research institute concluded in 2010 that, "the main reason talented people leave [the military] is not the lure of a lucrative civilian career, but because mediocre people stay in and get promoted."[45] Do not be mediocre and do not worry about promotion; take care of the leaders under you and they will carry you there. The Air Force asks a lot out of its people. The main avenue for Airmen to get something meaningful out of their service is you. Empower them, give them back their time, listen to their voice, and foster their pride.

---

[45] Ricks, *The Generals: American Military Command from World War II to Today*, 450.

About The Authors

Darrell Moyers: Captain Darrell Moyers has been an Air Force Flight Commander multiple times over and is a graduate of the Naval Postgraduate School. Captain Moyers has led Intelligence Flights of over one hundred Airmen, NCOs, Civilians, and Officers both in-garrison and in overseas combat zones.

Michael Parker: Major Michael Parker is a career Air Force Intelligence Officer, three-time wing senior intelligence officer, and was Flight Commander of a 135 member flight.

Julie Roloson: Major Julie Roloson is a Security Forces Squadron Commander, and has been a Flight Commander and Operations Officer in multiple assignments across the globe. She is also a CENTCOM FAO and a graduate of the Naval Postgraduate School.

Uwe Hartmann: Colonel Uwe Hartmann, Ph.D, is a German general staff officer with leadership experience from platoon to regiment level.

Each author and contributor bring over a decade of experience from their respective fields and levels of leadership. Their collective and diverse viewpoints are what give this document its true value.

References

US Airforce Public Affairs. "AF to Fund Squadron Innovation That Improves Mission Effectiveness," February 23, 2018. https://www.af.mil/News/Article-Display/Article/1448681/af-to-fund-squadron-innovation-that-improves-mission-effectiveness/.

Brandebo, Maria F, Johan Osterberg, and Anna K Berglund. "The Impact of Constructive and Destructive Leadership on Soldier's Job Satisfaction." *Psychological Reports*, Applied Psychology, 122, no. 3 (2019): 1068–86.

Canning, Natalie. "Empowering Communities Through Inspirational Leadership." In *Managing Early Years Settings: Supporting and Leading Teams*, edited by Alison Robins and Sue Callan. California: Sage, 2009.

Cohen, Eliot A. *Supreme Command: Soldiers, Statesmen, and Leadership in Wartime*. New York: Random House, 2002.

Dempsey, Martine E. "Mission Command White Paper." Joint Chiefs of Staff, April 3, 2012.

Dobelli, Rolf. *The Art of Thinking Clearly*. New York: HarperCollins Publishers, 2013.

Gates, Robert M. *Duty: Memoirs of a Secretary at War*. New York: Random House, 2014.

Guenzi, Paolo, and Dino Ruta. *Leading Teams: Tools and Techniques for Successful Team Leaders from the Sports World*. San Francisco: John Wiley & Sons Ltd, 2013.

Hedlund, Jennifer, Joseph Horvath, George Forsythe, Scott Snook, Wendy Williams, Richard Bullis, Martin Dennis, and Robert Sternberg. "Tacit Knowledge in Military Leadership: Evidence of Construct Validity." Technical. Yale University: United States Army Research Institute for the Behavioral and Social Sciences, 1998.

Kotter, John P. *Leading Change.* MA: Harvard Business Review, 2012.

Langley, John K. "Occupational Burnout and Retention of Air Force Distributed Common Ground System Intelligence Personnel." RAND Corporation, 2012.

Lewinska, Monika. "The Role of Communication in Military Leadership." *Journal of Corporate Responsibility and Leadership* 2, no. 1 (2015).

Lorenz, Stephen. *Lorenz on Leadership: Lessons on Effectively Leading People, Teams, and Organizations.* Maxwell AFB, Alabama: Air University Press, 2012.

Mance, Charles C, Craig L Pearce, and Henry P Sims. "The Ins and Outs of Leading Teams: An Overview," 2009.

McChrystal, Stanley. *My Share of the Task.* New Jersey: Penguin, 2013.

"Military Leadership Diversity Commission Decision Paper #3: Retention." Military Leadership Diversity Commission, February 2011.

Reilly, Bradley. "Eradicating Toxic Leadership." Columbus Air Force Base, June 2017. https://www.columbus.af.mil/News/Commentaries/Display/Article/1227533/eradicating-toxic-leadership/.

Ricks, Thomas E. *The Generals: American Military Command from World War II to Today*. New York: Random House, 2013.

Shultz, Richard. "Military Innovation in War: It Takes a Learning Organization, A Case Study of Task Force 714 in Iraq." Case Study. Florida: Joint Special Operations University, 2016.

Smiljanic, Drazen. "Transformational Military Leadership - Requirements, Characteristics and Development." *Czech Military Review* 25 (2015): 18–48.

Smith, Jeffry F. *Commanding an Air Force Squadron in the Twenty-First Century: A Practical Guide of Tips and Techniques for Today's Squadron Commander*. Alabama: Air University Press, 2003.

Velsor, Ellen V, Cynthia D McCauley, and Marian N Ruderman. *Handbook of Leadership Development*. 3rd ed. San Francisco: Jossey-Bass, 2010.

Woodward, Bob. *Obama's Wars*. New York: Simon & Schuster, 2010.

Carola Hartmann Miles-Verlag

<u>Schriften zur Tradition</u>

Eberhard Birk, Winfried Heinemann, Sven Lange (Hrsg.), *Tradition für die Bundeswehr. Neue Aspekte einer alten Debatte,* Berlin 2012.

Donald Abenheim, Uwe Hartmann (Hrsg.), *Tradition in der Bundeswehr. Zum Erbe des deutschen Soldaten und zur Umsetzung des neuen Traditionserlasses,* Berlin 2018.

Joachim Welz, *Vom Kontingentsheer zum Reichsheer: Militärkonventionen als Motor der Wehrverfassung,* Berlin 2018.

Donald Abenheim, Uwe Hartmann, *Einführung in die Tradition der Bundeswehr. Das soldatische Erbe in dem besten Deutschland, das es je gab,* Berlin 2019.

Eberhard Birk, Heiner Möllers (Hrsg.), *Die Luftwaffe und ihre Traditionen (aus der Reihe Schriften zur Geschichte der Deutschen Luftwaffe, Band 10),* Berlin 2019.

Hans-Günter Behrendt (Hrsg.), *Erinnerungsorte der Bundeswehr,* Berlin 2020.

<u>Erinnerungen</u>

Blue Braun, *Erinnerungen an die Marine 1956–1996,* Berlin 2012.

Klaus Grot, *So war's, damals. Dienstchronik eines Pionieroffiziers im Kalten Krieg 1954–1991,* Berlin 2014.

Gustav Lünenborg, *Bürger und Soldat. Innere Führung hautnah 1956–1993, 1993–2015,* Berlin 2015.

Adolf Brüggemann, *Als Offizier der Bundeswehr im Auswärtigen Dienst. Meine Erinnerungen als Militärattaché in Seoul (Republik Korea) 1978–83 und in Prag (Tschechoslowakei/Tschechien) 1988–1993,* Berlin 2015.

Rainer Buske, *Eine Reise ins Innere der Bundeswehr. Wundersame Geschichten aus einer anderen Welt*, Berlin 2016.

Heinz Laube, *Duell am Himmel*, Berlin 2016.

Viktor Toyka, *Dienst in Zeiten des Wandels. Erinnerungen aus 40 Jahren Dienst als Marineoffizier 1966-2000*, Berlin 2017.

Hans-Eckhard Tribess (Hrsg.), *Im Leben unterwegs – für den Frieden. Festschrift für Wolfgang Altenburg zum 90. Geburtstag am 22. Juni 2018*, Berlin 2019.

Kurt Graf v. Schweinitz, *Notizen im Transit von Krieg und Frieden*, Berlin 2020.

Militärgeschichte

Eberhard Kliem, Kathrin Orth, *"Wir wurden wie blödsinnig vom Feind beschossen". Menschen und Schiffe in der Skagerrakschlacht 1916*, Berlin 2016.

Hans Frank, Norbert Rath, *Kommodore Rudolf Petersen. Führer der Schnellboote 1942–1945. Ein Leben in Licht und Schatten unteilbarer Verantwortung*, Berlin 2016.

Eckhard Lisec, *Der Völkermord an den Armeniern im 1. Weltkrieg – Deutsche Offiziere beteiligt?*, Berlin 2017.

Ingo Pfeiffer, *Heinz Neukirchen. Marinekarriere an wechselnden Fronten*, Berlin 2017.

Joachim Welz, *Erfolgsstory oder Trauma – die Übernahme von Armeen. Lehren aus der Übernahme des österreichischen Bundesheeres in die Wehrmacht 1938 und der Reste der NVA in die Bundeswehr 1990*, Berlin 2018.

Joachim Hoppe, Manfred Wilde (Hrsg.), *Die Unteroffizierschule des Heeres, Die militärische Meisterschule*, Berlin 2016.

Georg Neuhaus, *Am Anfang war ein Speer. Eine Chronographie der Kriegs- und Militärtechnologien*, Berlin 2018.

Hans-Werner Ahrens, *Die Transportflieger der Luftwaffe 1956 bis 197. Konzeption – Aufbau – Einsatz, (Reihe Schriften zur Geschichte der Deutschen Luftwaffe, Band 8)*, Berlin 2019.

Jobst Reller, *Die Anfänge der evangelischen Militärseelsorge,* Berlin 2019.

Eberhard Frhr. v. Senden, Friedrich Frhr. v. Senden, *Der Erste Weltkrieg 1914–1918. Erlebnisse eines jungen Leutnants,* Berlin 2020

Einsatzerfahrungen

Artur Schwitalla, *Afghanistan, jetzt weiß ich erst… Gedanken aus meiner Zeit als Kommandeur des Provincial Reconstruction Team FEYZABAD,* Berlin 2010.

Rainer Buske, *KUNDUZ. Ein Erlebnisbericht über einen militärischen Einsatz der Bundeswehr in AFGHANISTAN im Jahre 2008,* Berlin ²2016.

Militär und Gesellschaft

Hans-Christian Beck, Christian Singer (Hrsg.), *Entscheiden – Führen – Verantworten. Soldatsein im 21. Jahrhundert,* Berlin 2011.

Wolf Graf von Baudissin, *Grundwert Frieden in Politik – Strategie – Führung von Streitkräften,* hrsg. von Claus von Rosen, Berlin 2014.

Marcel Bohnert, Lukas J. Reitstetter (Hrsg.), *Armee im Aufbruch. Zur Gedankenwelt junger Offiziere in den Kampftruppen der Bundeswehr,* Berlin 2014.

Phil C. Langer, Gerhard Kümmel (Hrsg.), *„Wir sind Bundeswehr." Wie viel Vielfalt benötigen/vertragen die Streitkräfte?,* Berlin 2015.

Eberhard Birk, Peter Andreas Popp (Hrsg.), *Luftwaffenoffizier 21. Das Selbstverständnis des Luftwaffenoffiziers zu Beginn des 21. Jahrhunderts, (aus der Reihe Schriften zur Geschichte der Deutschen Luftwaffe, Band 5),* Berlin 2016.

Alois Bach, Walter Sauer (Hrsg.), *Schützen.Retten.Kämpfen. Dienen für Deutschland,* Berlin 2016.

Marcel Bohnert, Björn Schreiber (Hrsg.), *Die unsichtbaren Veteranen. Kriegsheimkehrer in der deutschen Gesellschaft,* Berlin 2016.

Angelika Dörfler-Dierken (Hrsg.), *Hinschauen! Geschlecht, Rechtspopulismus, Rituale: Systemische Probleme oder individuelles Fehlverhalten?,* Berlin 2019.

Jahrbuch Innere Führung (seit 2009)

Uwe Hartmann, Claus von Rosen (Hrsg.), *Jahrbuch Innere Führung 2018. Innere Führung zwischen Aufbruch, Abbau und Abschaffung: Neues denken, Mitgestaltung fördern, Alternativen wagen,* Berlin 2018.

Uwe Hartmann, Claus von Rosen (Hrsg.), *Jahrbuch Innere Führung 2019. Bundeswehr im Aufbruch. Hindernisse von den verteidigungspolitischen Vorstellungen der AFD bis zu den sicherheitspolitischen Meinungen in der Zivilgesellschaft,* Berlin 2019.

Standpunkte und Orientierungen

Daniel Giese, *Militärische Führung im Internetzeitalter,* Berlin 2014.

Dirk Freudenberg, *Auftragstaktik und Innere Führung. Feststellungen und Anmerkungen zur Frage nach Bedeutung und Verhältnis des inneren Gefüges und der Auftragstaktik unter den Bedingungen des Einsatzes der Deutschen Bundeswehr,* Berlin 2014.

Hartwig von Schubert, *Integrative Militärethik. Ethische Urteilsbildung in der militärischen Führung,* Berlin 2015.

Uwe Hartmann, *Hybrider Krieg als neue Bedrohung von Freiheit und Frieden. Zur Relevanz der Inneren Führung in Politik, Gesellschaft und Streitkräften,* Berlin 2015.

Klaus Beckmann, *Treue.Bürgermut.Ungehorsam. Anstöße zur Führungskultur und zum beruflichen Selbstverständnis in der Bundeswehr,* Berlin 2015.

Florian Beerenkämper, Marcel Bohnert, Anja Buresch, Sandra Matuszewski, *Der innerafghanische Friedens- und Aussöhnungsprozess*, Berlin 2016.

Martin Sebaldt, *Nicht abwehrbereit. Die Kardinalprobleme der deutschen Streitkräfte, der Offenbarungseid des Weißbuchs und die Wege aus der Gefahr*, Berlin 2017.

Christian J. Grothaus, *Der „hybride Krieg" vor dem Hintergrund der kollektiven Gedächtnisse Estlands, Lettlands und Litauens*, Berlin 2017.

Uwe Hartmann, *Der gute Soldat. Politische Kultur und soldatisches Selbstverständnis heute*, Berlin 2018.

Christian Bauer, Marcel Bohnert, Jan Pahl, *Vitalis Innere Führung! Zum Status Quo der Führungskultur in den deutschen Streitkräften*, Berlin 2018.

Helmut Jermer, *Innere Führung kompakt. Eine Zusammenschau als Lehr- und Lernhilfe*, Berlin 2019.

<u>Monterey Studies</u>

Donald Abenheim, *Soldier and Politics Transformed*, Berlin 2007.

Michael G. Lux, *Innere Führung – A Superior Concept of Leadership?*, Berlin 2009.

Jochen Wittmann, *Auftragstaktik*, Berlin 2012.

Grégoire Monnet, *The Evolution of Strategic Thought Since September 11, 2001*, Berlin 2016.

Stefan Klein, *America First? Isolationism in U.S. Foreign Policy from the 19th to the 21st Century*, Berlin 2017.

Torsten Gojowsky, Sebastian Kögler, *Building Special Operations Relationships with Fragile Partners. Best practices from Iraq, Syria, and Afghanistan*, Berlin 2019.

www.miles-verlag.jimdo.com